OUIJA BOARD ENIGMA

Title: Ouija Board Enigma
Genre: Non-Fiction
Desc: Is the Ouija Board real or fake? Is it a tool for communication with spirits, a tool to access our inner most thoughts, or a mere device for entertainment? This book views the origins and evolution of the Ouija board and the various cultures that have used the Ouija board throughout history.
Author: Kambiz Mostofizadeh
Publisher: Mikazuki Publishing House
ISBN-13: 9781942825111
Date Published: July 2016

OUIJA BOARD ENIGMA

TABLE OF CONTENTS

OUIJA BOARD ENIGMA

WHAT'S THE OUIJA BOARD?

A question that has been an enigma for scientists, scholars, philosophers, researchers, intellectuals, Ouija Board experts, and spiritualists and this is the ultimate question of

OUIJA BOARD ENIGMA

this book. Is the Ouija board a real method for communication with spirits? Is it the human's tool for tapping in to the subconscious and drawing out memories that have been blocked and hidden? Or is it just a harmless pastime for entertainment? There are many researchers that believe that the Talking Board also known as the Spirit Board or Ouija Board, was first created by Pythagoras in 540 B.C. Greece as well as parts of Asia Minor, believed in the use of oracles to predict the future. What is a spirit? A spirit or apparition is believed to be an energy that does not have a physical being. This energy, known by most humans as your spirit, is measurable and readable using an EMF meter or Electromagnetic Frequency meter and other energy sensing/measuring devices. This is known as kinetic energy or moving energy. Interestingly enough, the German word for kinetic energy is poltergeist.

OUIJA BOARD ENIGMA

Kinetic energy is measurable therefore the
EMF metering method used to reach the result
is scientific. Why were these EMF devices
built? For construction purposes mostly, but
ghost hunters have adapted the use of the
EMF meter for reading energy signals. Energy
that is measured is quantifiable, making it
scientific. The Talking Board or Ouija Board,
was viewed by the Greeks as an oracle. The
Oracle at Delphi is one such example. An
oracle is a medium (person) that answers
questions posed to it by an individual. The
Ouija Board was not created by spiritualists,
but rather capitalists that sought to capitalize
on the popularity of spiritualism in the 1800's.
The Ouija Board, was viewed as a sort of an
oracle, but in an entertaining fashion rather
than as a serious device for fortune telling.
Epes Sargent in 1869 wrote that "When the

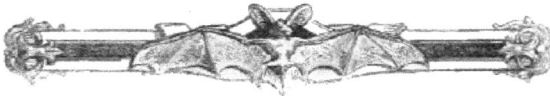

OUIJA BOARD ENIGMA

modern rapping phenomena began to be

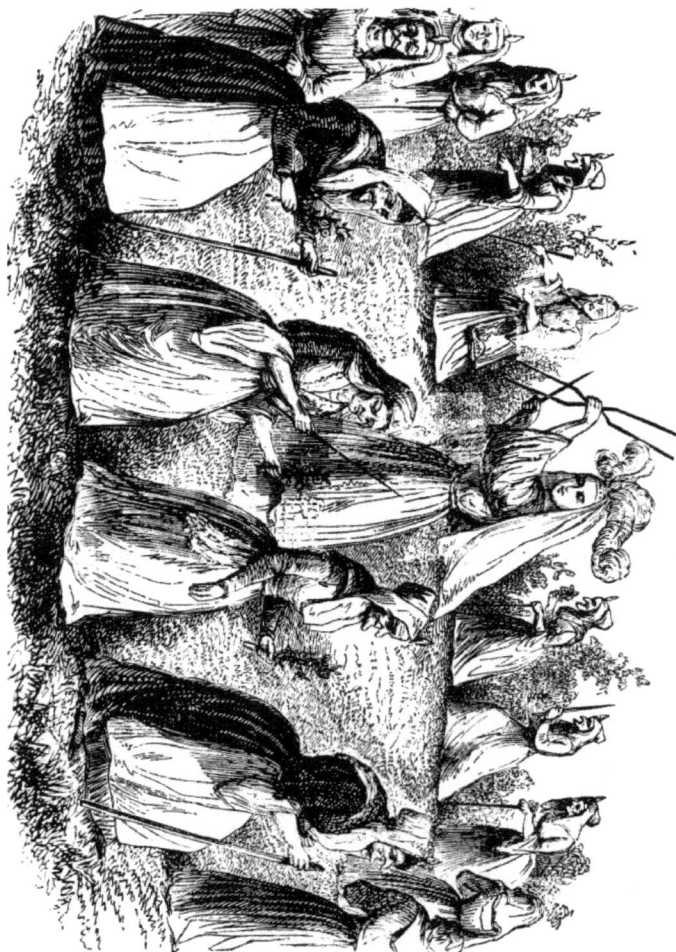

OUIJA BOARD ENIGMA

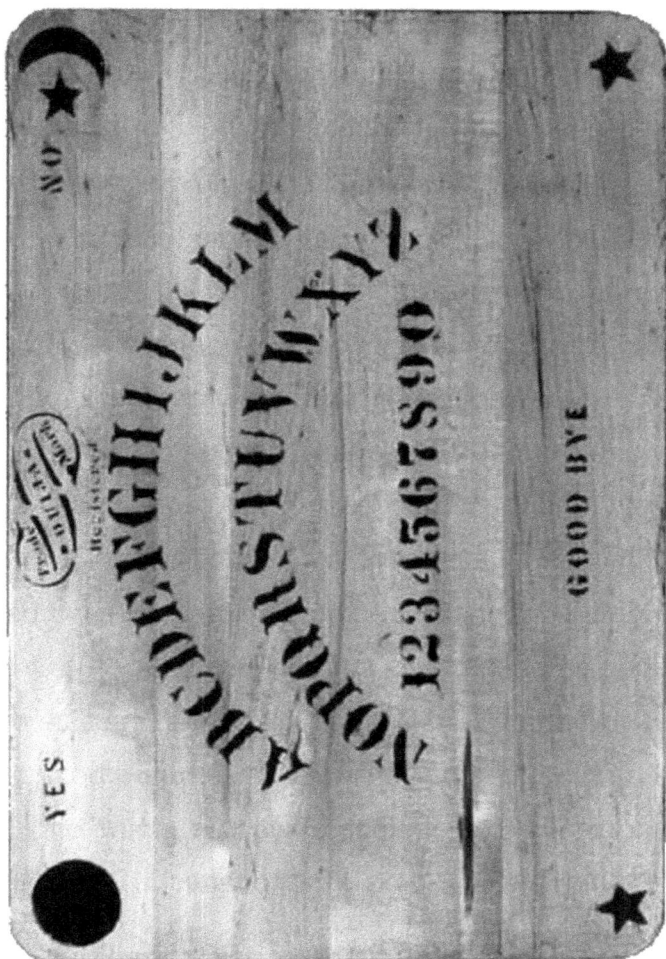

Original design of the Ouija Board

investigated, communications were received by the tedious process of calling over the alphabet, and noting down the letters at which the rap was given. Then, when the movements of tables took place, it was suggested that by arranging a pencil at the foot of a light table, and placing a sheet of paper under it, the intelligent force that was operating might produce written sentences. The device was tried, and found successful. The table, once set in motion by the passive influence of a medium, began to trace characters, then words and sentences. This method was finally simplified by substituting little tables, the size of a hand; then small baskets, pasteboard boxes, and finally the flat piece of wood, running on little wheels, and called Planchette."

Up until that point, the planchette had a hole in the top of it where a lead pencil was inserted.

Ouija Boards Are Sporting Goods, Rules Court

WASHINGTON, June 5. — The supreme court today announced it would not determine what is a ouija board.

The question was presented in a case brought by the Baltimore Talking Board Company, which protested against taxation of such boards as sporting goods, and insisted that should the court refuse to hold that the board "is a grade of motor autoism, involving considerable subconscious action of intelligence," that it should at least classify the smaller boards as "children's toys"

The lower federal courts sustained the government's contention that the boards should be classed as sporting goods.

Bisbee Daily Review. (Bisbee, Ariz), June 06, 1922

OUIJA BOARD ENIGMA

Norman Rockwell's famous drawing

The creation of the Ouija Board removed the pencil from the top and the planchette was used as a selector of letters on the board. When the Kennard Novelty company created and registered the Ouija board in 1891, it was

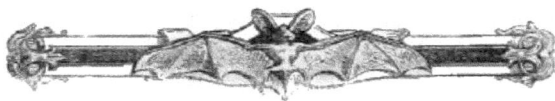

OUIJA BOARD ENIGMA

thought of as entertainment. Fuld registered over 20 trademarks and patents and sent countless letters to copycats, warning them to stop counterfeiting his unique creation. The name that William Fuld used "Ouija" is a combination of two French and German words. "Oui" meaning "yes" in French and "Ja" meaning "yes" in German. But what is it really William Fuld's creation? Although his officially registered trademarks and patents indicate so, the Ouija board is much older than William Fuld. Before the entertainment device that William Fuld purchased the patent to was titled the "Ouija board", the Ouija board had in fact been used with the name of "Spirit Board." According to the Library of Congress "In 1890, while conducting a séance at the Langham Hotel in Baltimore, Maryland, Elijah Bond, Charles Kennard, and Helen Peters ask the board they are developing what it wants to be

OUIJA BOARD ENIGMA

called. It mysteriously answers "O-U-I-J-A".
When asked what the word means it responds
with "G-O-O-D—L-U-C-K". Bond and Kennard
incorporate the Kennard Novelty Company and
begin manufacturing the Ouija board in
Baltimore. In 1891, William Fuld buys the rights
to the game and records a patent. In 1901, the
Ouija Novelty Company revokes the license to
make Ouija from William Fuld's brother, Isaac,
beginning a nineteen-year court battle. Isaac
tries to continue making Ouija, but is stopped
by a court order. In 1915, Pearl Curran, a St.
Louis Missouri housewife, uses the board to
contact Patience Worth, a 17th-cenury New

OUIJA BOARD ENIGMA

England literary figure. She transcribes her writings and publishes several of her plays, poems, and short stories. In 1920, after nineteen years of legal wrangling, the courts confirm that only William Fuld has the right to manufacture Ouija boards. They rule against his brother Isaac, making him pay court costs." Famous artist Norman Rockwell painted a famous magazine cover featuring a couple at home, playing on the Ouija board. Lewis Spence in 1920 wrote in his book the

OUIJA BOARD ENIGMA

Encyclopedia of Occultism that "Another form is the Ouija board on which in a convenient order the letters of the alphabet are printed and over which a pointer easily moves under the direction of the hand of the person or persons acting as mediums. It is stated that a form of this "mystic toy" was in use in the days of Pythagoras, about 540 B.C. In a French history of Pythagoras, the author describing his celebrated school of philosophy, asserts that the brother- hood held frequent séances in circles at which a mystic table, moving on wheels, moved towards signs inscribed on the surface of a stone slab on which the moving-table worked. The author states that probably Pythagoras, in his travels among the Eastern nations, observed some such apparatus in use amongst them and adapted his idea from them. Another trace of some such "communicating mechanism" is found in

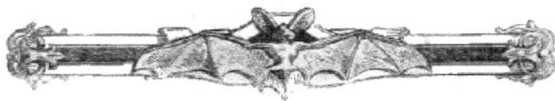

OUIJA BOARD ENIGMA

the Scandinavian legend how the people of in

the twelfth century had a high priest, one whose predictions were renowned for their accuracy throughout the length and breadth of the land. He had in his possession a little ivory doll that drew with "a pointed instrument" on parchment or "other substance," certain signs to which the priest had the key. The

OUIJA BOARD ENIGMA

communications were in every case prophetic
utterances, and it is said in every case came

true. The writer who recounts the legend
thought it probable that the priest had procured
the doll in China. America in the mid to late 19th
century and early 20th century, experienced a

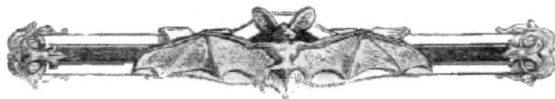

OUIJA BOARD ENIGMA

surge in the popularity of spiritualism. People actively sought out and hosted mediums that claimed to have the ability to contact spirits. A craze overtook certain elements in the East Coast aristocratic establishment, causing them to support spiritualism. All sorts of mediums appeared claiming super-human powers and

OUIJA BOARD ENIGMA

the ability to communicate with the dead.
Famous escape artist and Magician Harry
Houdini became an outspoken critic, proving
that the mediums of the day were using
gimmicks and methods that were known by
illusionists and magicians. Houdini used the
media to challenge mediums to prove that they
could speak with the dead. Headlines on the
advertising of his shows stated "Houdini
Exposes Fraud Mediums". Houdini took
interest in one medium that was gaining in
popularity in the East Coast named Margery.
Margery like other mediums, claimed that she
could in fact communicate with the dead.
Margery would claim that when she
communicated with spirits, liquid named
ectoplasm would exit from her mouth and ears.
Even Scientific American, a popular American
scientific magazine, was taken by the
American craze of spiritualism, and offered a

OUIJA BOARD ENIGMA

large sum of money to anyone that could prove that they could communicate with the dead. Not one medium was able to prove that they held any power to communicate with the dead, but many mediums came forward claiming they could. Houdini saw it as a personal mission to prove that mediums and spiritualists were frauds and Margery became a subject of his energies.

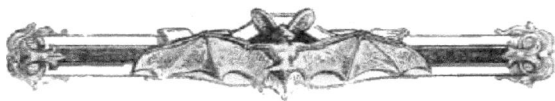

OUIJA BOARD ENIGMA

About one of his "séances" with Margery aka Mina Crandon, Harry Houdini wrote the following:

"On the evening in question the bell-box was placed between my feet with my right foot between it and Mrs. Crandon's left foot. As the séance progressed I could distinctly feel her ankle slowly and spasmodically sliding as it pressed against mine while she gained space to raise her foot off the floor and touch the top of the box. To the ordinary sense of touch the contract would seem the same while this was

OUIJA BOARD ENIGMA

being done. At times she would say: 'Just press hard against my ankle so you can see that my ankle is there,' and as she pressed I could feel her gain another half inch. When she had finally maneuvered her foot around to a point where she could get at the top of the box the bell ringing began and I positively felt the tendons of her leg flex and tighten as she repeatedly touched the ringing apparatus. There is no question in my mind about it. She did this. Then, when the ringing was over, I

OUIJA BOARD ENIGMA

plainly felt her leg slide back into its original position with her foot on the floor beside mine." Instead of Houdini being hailed as a hero for exposing the frauds and con-artists posing as so-called mediums, Houdini was attacked by many mediums during his life and after his death. It appears the mediums were more interested in smearing the name of Houdini, rather than seeking the truth about communication with the other world. Famed author of Sherlock Holmes, Sir Arthur Conan Doyle, was also a spiritualist that believed that humans held the ability to communicate with the dead. His belief in the ability of mediums may have been more related to his drive to generate money than an actual motive of discovering the truth. His promotion of Spiritualism was partially successful, because his name as a famous author had been

OUIJA BOARD ENIGMA

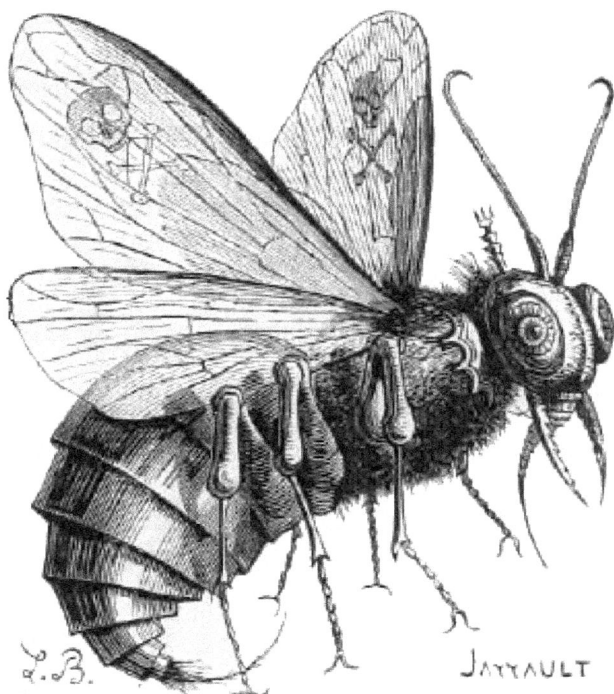

cemented by his creation of Sherlock Holmes. As of this writing, there has not yet been one case of a medium being able to prove, beyond a shadow of a doubt that they are able to communicate with spirits or entities from another dimension. The mediums that have become popular were individuals that enriched

OUIJA BOARD ENIGMA

themselves through duping and fooling innocent individuals using a combination of clever patter, stagecraft techniques, and lighting to fool the (paying) spectators. Mediums were copying and incorporating the techniques created by illusionists and magicians in order to "trick" everyone watching. Using an old method created by magicians, the medium would have "confederates" or helpers in the crowd that would help the medium by making noises and creating general disturbances in order to add to the atmosphere. One helper would use his knee under the table to lift the table while another helper made noises over the voice of the speaking medium. These sessions to contact spirits were labeled as "Séances" and séances became a popular occurrence as a form of entertainment for the rich. These séances and attempts at communication with spirits by

OUIJA BOARD ENIGMA

mediums became so popular that small and large theaters in America and Europe began to host shows themed around them. The use of early stage lighting techniques and glass slides created primitive holography which allowed for the projection of apparition or spirit-like images to be seen by public (paying) audiences. Even

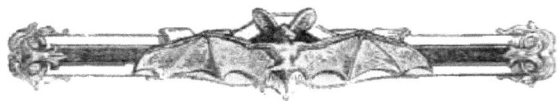

OUIJA BOARD ENIGMA

magicians began to advertise séances and communication with spirits in their shows. Fearing that they would be called liars and charlatans, many magicians kept up the story of their ability to communicate with spirits, even when not on the stage. From authors, magicians, to con-artists, people that were set to derive even some economic benefit from the rise of spiritualism and mediums, began to support the claim of communication with spirits. A gullible public flocked in droves to theaters to see the séances and many women fainted from the sight of spirits manufactured through stage lighting techniques. In present times, it is easy to tell when a CGI effect or computer animation is being used in a movie to generate a background or an animated character. In the early 20th century, the sight of a fake spirit would have been shocking, disturbing, and frightening. Mainstream America became

OUIJA BOARD ENIGMA

enthralled with the Ouija Board after I Love Lucy, a wildly popular TV show, featured an episode in 1951 with Lucy and Ethel doing a séance using a Ouija Board. This particular episode pushed the Ouija Board in to the

mainstream and popular culture. The Exorcist, one of the most famous horror movies of all

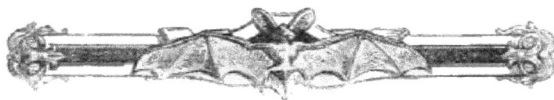

OUIJA BOARD ENIGMA

time, based its story around a 12 year old girl that is possessed by a demon after playing alone with a Ouija Board. Horror movie film makers and production companies picked up on the Ouija Board craze and movies were created like Witchboard and Ouija that based their stories around demonic possession from Ouija Board use.

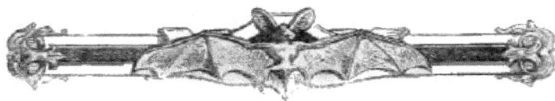

OUIJA BOARD ENIGMA

Witchboard premiered in 1986 and was made with an estimated 2 million dollar budget. The movie grossed over 7 million dollars at the box office and made at least 3 million dollars in video sales and licensing. The movie was wildly popular and helped to make sales of the Ouija Board skyrocket in the 1980's. Witchboard was not only a horror movie based around the spirit board but also gave viewers vital information on how to use the board itself. The movie was centered around a woman that had become obsessed with using the Ouija Board alone, make her open to demonic possession and influence. The movie shows her going through the stages of "Progressive Entrapment", which included her experiencing symptoms that were revealing her gradual possession by an evil spirit. The brought the Ouija Board in to the forefront and mainstream of the 1980's and helped to cement its position

OUIJA BOARD ENIGMA

as one of the greatest selling board games of all time.

JUST A NOVELTY

The Kennard Novelty company in the late 1800's began advertising a spirit board, also known as a talking board or Ouija Board. The spiritualism craze of the mid to late 1800's fueled the creation such a product, and the Ouija Board was wildly successful in making sales. In 1890, William H. A. Maupin, Harry Welles Rusk, Colonel Washington Bowie, Charles W. Kennard, and John F. Green created the Kennard Novelty company. In 1892, the company was re-organized as the Ouija Novelty Company with William Fuld, a former Kennard Novelty company employee, becoming its President. Kennard left after a few years and started manufacturing another talking board called the Volo, that was to be in

OUIJA BOARD ENIGMA

competition with the Ouija Novelty Company's patented Ouija Board. Kennard is believed by

many to have been the original creator of the Ouija Board because it was he that brought together a group of investors to being the company, but differences in opinion with his business partners, may be the reason that he left the company which he had originally started. By creating the Volo talking board, Kennard could now make his own decisions as

OUIJA BOARD ENIGMA

to the future of this product. Unfortunately for Kennard, his success was short-lived, as the Volo was manufactured for less than 6 months. The Ouija Novelty company sued Kennard for infringement and the Volo stopped being manufactured all together. The Kennard Novelty company which later became the Ouija Novelty Company, went on to sell the Ouija Board patent to Parker Brothers in 1966. In 1967, the Ouija Board sold 2 million units, shockingly outselling Monopoly, which is still to this day one of the greatest selling board games of all time. Hasbro went on to purchase Parker Brothers, giving them control and ownership over the trademark, patent, and design of the Ouija Board. Ouija is the registered and patented name owned by Hasbro. Despite their being millions of spirit boards aka talking boards aka Ouija Boards sold, and there having been cases where

OUIJA BOARD ENIGMA

crimes were committed and attributed to the use of the Ouija Board, there has never been an authentic and scientifically proven case or incident that can show that the Ouija Board is anything other than a device for entertainment. As far as the manufacturers and most of the users of it are concerned, it is an entertainment device used to pass the time.

PSYCHIC WRITING

Psychic writing also became a popular phenomenon, as mediums turned to the use of the pen to supposedly contact spirits. The medium would hold a pen in his or her hand while asking questions from a supposed spirit.

OUIJA BOARD ENIGMA

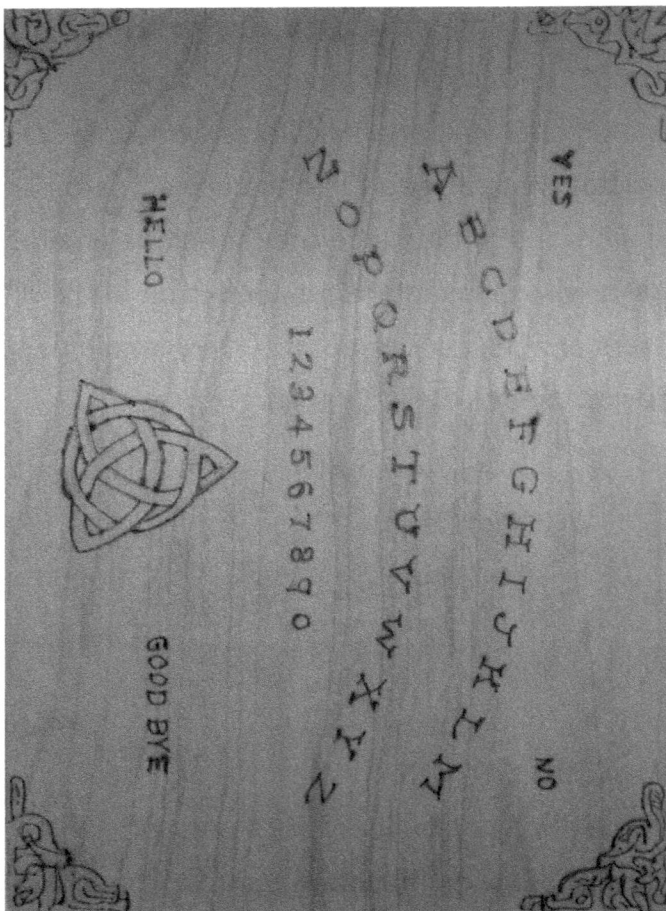

Handmade Talking Board aka Ouija Board

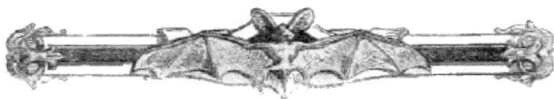

OUIJA BOARD ENIGMA

The spirit or some supernatural force, would supposedly control the hand of the medium, causing them to write, scribble, doodle, or

OUIJA BOARD ENIGMA

draw. The scribblings were then analyzed and deciphered as to their meaning, itself a vague and abstract process. It was supposedly supernatural forces that was giving the mediums messages through the writing device. Was there a spirit or supernatural force actually controlling the hand of the medium? It is again, like the use of the Ouija Board, a matter of the subconscious mind causing automatic muscular movements, creating the illusion of writing. Most of the time, any scribbling or writing is un-intelligible. Automatons were even created featuring Psychic Writing. After the medium had written down all that he/she was to write down, the written down text or art was then interpreted as being a message from a spirit. The medium and the spectators accepted the writings as de facto proof of their being a spirit in control of the medium's pen. It

OUIJA BOARD ENIGMA

was never proven to be anything other than pure entertainment, but the popularity of it spread to metropolitan cities and it became commonplace in the early 20th century. Automatons were even created that sought to copy the automatic writing or psychic writing phenomenon. Ideomotor activity caused the pencil to write down messages but these messages were then interpreted by a person, making the messages second-hand and meaningless. If they did suddenly take on some meaning, it is because the person reading the messages was injecting their own perspective and viewpoint in to it, making them appear to be something that they were not.

OUIJA BOARD ENIGMA

MY MOST RECENT EXPERIENCE

I bought a Ouija board from a toy store and brought it home. Opened the box, took out the board, and invited two witnesses to join me. I

also purchased a simple EMF Meter or Electro-Magnetic Frequency meter, and placed it at the

OUIJA BOARD ENIGMA

top of the Ouija board (OB). Below is the transcript of the voice recorded session.

Me: We are starting our session. Is there anyone here right now? If you here now, make a sign.

(The EMF Meter started making noise.)

Me: We are getting EMF activity.

(The EMF Meter started making noise.)

Me: The EMF Meter is making noise and the Ouija board planchette is moving. Do I have confirmation on EMF activity?

Witness 1: Yes

Me: What is your name?

(Planchette moving to letters)

OB: S-A-T-A-N

(The EMF Meter started making noise.)

Me: We are getting EMF activity. Do I have confirmation?

Witness 1: Yes

Me: Have you been in this house before?

OUIJA BOARD ENIGMA

Drawing of the demon Zozo (Pazuzu)

(The EMF Meter started making noise.)

Me: We are getting EMF activity. When was the last time you were in this house?

OB: 9 days ago

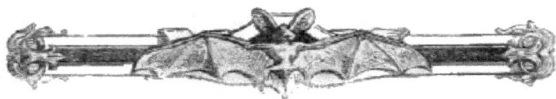

OUIJA BOARD ENIGMA

Me: What is your real name?

OB: Z-O-Z-O

Me: Zozo. It was Zozo from the beginning.

(The EMF Meter started making noise.)

Me: We are getting EMF activity. Are we safe using the Ouija board?

OB: No

Me: Who is going to bother us using the Ouija board?

OB: M-A-M-A

Me: Who is controlling the Ouija board right now?

OB: M-A-M-A

(The EMF Meter started making noise.)

Me: We are getting EMF activity. Do I have confirmation?

Witness 1: Yes

Me: When will I get married?

OB: 20 months

Me: 20 months?

OUIJA BOARD ENIGMA

(The EMF Meter started making noise.)

Me: We are getting heavy EMF activity. Is Donald Trump going to become President?

OB: No

Me: What's the price of Gold going to go up to?

OB: 2,000 dollars an ounce

Me: When? Tell me.

OB: 16 months

OUIJA BOARD ENIGMA

Me: Is America going to become a cashless society? How many years from now?

OB: 7 years

Me: Do Aliens exist?

'OB: Yes

Me: Was witness 2 abducted by an alien?

OB: Yes

Me: Did they take her in a UFO?

OB: Yes

Me: Did they use her DNA to make a baby?

OB: Yes

Me: We are getting EMF activity. Does Atlantis exist?

OB: No

Me: Does the Loch Ness Monster exist?

OB: Yes

Me: Do Short Grey Aliens exist?

OB: Yes

Me: Is Obama an alien?

OB: No.

OUIJA BOARD ENIGMA

Me: Is oil going to become $1000 a barrel?

OB: Yes

Me: How many years from now?

OB: 7

Me: Go to goodbye. Time to say goodbye.

(Planchette moved to goodbye)

(The planchette moved towards the goodbye and I removed the planchette off the board)

Me: Session ended. 26 minutes long.

OUIJA BOARD ENIGMA

OUIJA BOARD ENIGMA

Clay model of a sheep's liver
used in divination (Babylon, c. 2,000 B.C.)

Exorcizing demons of disease (Babylon)

A Babylonian demon
(British Museum, No. 22458)

OUIJA BOARD ENIGMA

Ten Observations:

1. The EMF meter would make noise every time the planchette began to move quickly.
2. Raising my voice when asking questions caused the EMF meter at the top of the OB to make louder noises.
3. The OB was able to answer the majority of the questions, but not all the questions.
4. Some of the answers given by the OB were confusing or gibberish.
5. Questions asked of the OB were questions that dealt with legends, mysteries, and future events.
6. The OB was quick to answer questions.
7. The planchette moved faster based on the intensity of the question.
8. The OB delivered short answers.

OUIJA BOARD ENIGMA

9. The OB gave clear answers and did not answer vaguely.

10. The OB's planchette, when moved towards the EMF meter, caused the EMF meter to make noise.

The 26 minute session of using the Ouija board I conducted with two witnesses, was done in a sober and serious manner. Questions were

OUIJA BOARD ENIGMA

asked of the Ouija board and it responded quickly and concisely. I asked the Ouija board to make future predictions which it did, giving me direct and non-vague answers to my questions. The EMF meter made noise on and off, throughout the entire session. Because spirits are thought to be made of energy,

OUIJA BOARD ENIGMA

moving energy or kinetic energy, is thought to comprise a spirit's makeup. The EMF is believed by ghost hunters and spiritualists to represent a non-biased and scientific method for reading moving energy in a given area.

OUIJA BOARD ENIGMA

Zozo is believed by OB experts to be a 5000 year old Babylonian demon. Mama is also believed to be a Babylonian demon that is stronger than Zozo and is believed to take over many of the OB sessions. According to the

OUIJA BOARD ENIGMA

Dictionaire Infernal, in 1816 in France, there were reports that a girl named Tilly was possessed by Mama, Zozo, and a demon named Grapoulet. In this OB session, at first, Zozo was claiming to be Satan, but gave his name as Zozo after being pressured to do so. In the beginning of its use, the OB was claiming to be controlled by Mama, instead of Zozo. After I asked Zozo to come back on to the OB, the OB responded thereon as Zozo. Zozo is believed by Ouija board experts as a very powerful demon that has the ability to move physical objects, sexually harass, and torment, people that have contacted him. The Zozo phenomenon is unique to the Ouija board community and has been not only been an enigma unto itself but also has become a popular theme in spiritualist themed movies like Witchboard, I am Zozo, and Ouija.

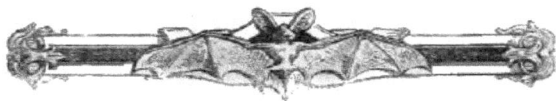

OUIJA BOARD ENIGMA

Astrologer being executed in 1602

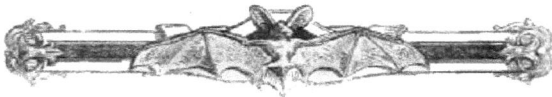

OUIJA BOARD ENIGMA

The popular theme, whether using the name Zozo or Mama or any other name, is that of an ancient demon or evil spirit, that is out to possess and destroy anyone that has come in contact with it. The only measurable and accurate device I know of that is able to read moving energy is an EMF. The EMF I was using was placed at the top of the Ouija board and made noises during specific times such as when I asked questions forcefully and when the planchette moved. As I was certain of myself and certain of the two witnesses with me, I am 100% positive and I am willing to take any lie detector test put in front of me, that I did not at any time purposefully move the planchette on the OB. I am 100% positive that the planchette of the OB was moving on its own. But why does the planchette of the OB move? Is it really a spirit that is moving the planchette or is there an easier and more

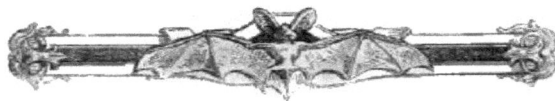

OUIJA BOARD ENIGMA

logical explanation for its movement?

IF IT'S NOT REAL, HOW DOES IT MOVE?

The planchette moves because of ideomotor activity in your body. Ideomotor is a combination of two words and that is idea and motor (muscular movement). The belief by psychologists is that your ideas and thoughts unconsciously power muscular movements,

OUIJA BOARD ENIGMA

causing the planchette on the Ouija Board to move. The planchette on the OB moves because your muscles are moving, even when you are resting your hands on the planchette.

OUIJA BOARD ENIGMA

The belief that the planchette on the OB is being moved by your own system's muscular movements could be an example of Occam's Razor, which states that the simplest explanation is the most correct one. Which is more likely? Your muscular movements are

OUIJA BOARD ENIGMA

pushing through your fingertips causing the planchette of the OB to move or you are speaking with a 5000 year old demon that is able to move physical objects? I would lean towards the simplest explanation which is that the planchette moves because of your muscular movements. If the person you are supposedly communicating with in the other world was real, would you not seek to know everything about the future? Indeed the OB did attempt to answer many questions about the future posed to it, but unless the events

actually occur with accuracy as answered by

the OB, it is difficult to say with certainty that
the OB actually knows anything more than
what you know. In other words, because your
fingers are connected to the planchette that is
resting on the OB, it is safe to say that any
answer you receive from the OB is an answer

OUIJA BOARD ENIGMA

already known to you or to one of the people touching the planchette. The reason is that the OB is really just giving answers that are hidden within the subconscious of one of the persons with their hand on the planchette. The scientific belief is that the OB is not a tool for supernatural communication, but rather a tool for subconscious navigation. This is why when you use the OB, you begin to see a pattern emerging. The OB can never answer a question whose answer is unknown to you and if it does answer, the answer will be gibberish, non-intelligible, and inaccurate. Using the principle of Occam's Razor, the simplest explanation for the OB is that it is your thoughts and subconscious are causing muscular movements that is moving the planchette and the answers you receive from the OB are answers already known to you or

OUIJA BOARD ENIGMA

J ALLAULT

one of the participants. According to Dr. William Benjamin Carpenter and his document written for the Royal Institution of Great Britain in 1852, argues that automatic muscular movements are the reason that the planchette is moving. He argued that it is ideomotor actions or bodily actions influenced by one's

OUIJA BOARD ENIGMA

own thoughts that are causing the planchette on the Ouija Board to move. It is indeed logical that the smallest amount of movement by a muscle could cause a lightweight planchette to move. This would further explain why the Ouija Board results in almost un-clear and un-intelligible messages nearly half the time it is being used. According to American psychologist Ray Hyman, "Honest, intelligent people can unconsciously engage in muscular activity that is consistent with their expectations." Hyman believes that individuals engaging in such activities such as spiritualism, tend to attribute ideomotor activity to spirits and external forces, instead of attributing it to their own actions. Hyman believes that it is automatic muscular movement that is responsible for the movement of the lightweight planchette.

OUIJA BOARD ENIGMA

REAL LIFE INCIDENTS

According to the June 23rd, 2014 article in the Daily Mail newspaper titled "Three American friends hospitalized after becoming 'possessed' following Ouija board game in Mexican village", three Mexican-Americans; Alexandra Huerta, her male cousin, and his friend Fernando Cuevas, were taken to the hospital to be treated after they experienced deafness, blindness , and hallucinations, after playing with the Ouija Board. Alexandra, was laughing frantically, growling, and was in a trance like state. The video of the incident was released on the Daily Mail website and is shocking and disturbing to the viewer. It shows an unbalanced and out of control young woman that had to have her entire body and head restrained, to prevent her from hurting herself and others around her. Did a demon possess her? It is difficult to diagnose a matter if you

OUIJA BOARD ENIGMA

Crystal balls were used as a fortune-telling device

are just dealing with the symptoms. What did in fact happen is that Alexandra, age 16, and her brother and friend, took Brugmansia or Angel's Trumpet, which is a very powerful

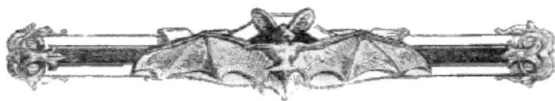

hallucinogenic substance from Latin America. .
It cannot be said with any certainty what
happened to them because humans are not
able to see the supernatural world. We can
only deal with what we see. What the
guardians of Alexandra saw and what the
paramedics saw, was a hysterical and growling
young woman on a hardcore hallucinogenic
that caused her to need medical attention.

SALEM

On March 1st, 1692, the Salem Witch Trials
began with the charging of Sarah Goode,
Sarah Osborne, and a Native American woman
named Tituba with witchcraft. It was said they
were behaving in an erratic manner and were
experiencing trances that no one could explain.
In the city of Salem, Massachusetts, hysteria
had developed about the appearance of
witches. Everyone became suspicious about

OUIJA BOARD ENIGMA

the existence of witches and their supposed
control over society. This incident became
famous around the world and is still the most
famous American incident regarding the

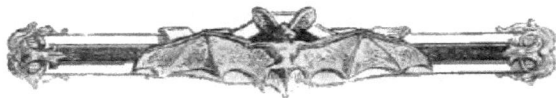

OUIJA BOARD ENIGMA

persecution of spiritualists. Many men and women were accused of being confederates of the Devil and working for the forces of evil. Accusations were made regarding the use of black magic, witchcraft, and of course divination. People were burned at the stake and their belongings, including their real estate were confiscated for the community. Were these people that were burned at the stake actual witches part of a witch's coven? Unless you are now a witch or have been a witch in the past, how do you know what a witch is? There may have been a few individuals playing with occult related items which resulted in their being accused of witchcraft. But it is difficult to believe that large numbers of the population of a city or town had turned to witchcraft. The modern theories include the "Hallucination Theory" and the "Economic Theory". The Hallucination Theory is that some of the people

OUIJA BOARD ENIGMA

of Salem were eating rotten bread, which was turning in to Lysergic Acid or LSD, causing them to hallucinate and to carry themselves in a paranoid state. The Economic Theory is that there existed internal conflicts over land and property amongst the denizens of Salem,

causing them to use the accusation of witchcraft to solve their legal problems. Being accused of witchcraft was frightening and created an atmosphere of conformity in the community of Salem. If you got in to a disagreement with your neighbor, your neighbor's grievances would have to be settled, or else you could be accused of witchcraft, resulting in your property and life being seized by the State. The false accusations of witchcraft were used as a political and economic tool in order for those that were levelling the accusations, to financially gain. The execution of a member of the community, made the community richer, and in many instances made the accuser richer. A simple land border dispute could be settled by claiming your neighbor was a witch, resulting in them being tortured and murdered by a community-sanctioned public execution.

OUIJA BOARD ENIGMA

The majority of persons accused of witchcraft in the Salem Witch Trials were women

OUIJA BOARD ENIGMA

The tortures included having huge heavy stones layed on or across your body "pressing" you in to a confession. Not surprisingly, many of the accused died under this torture. The accused were given one or sometimes several tests to determine if they are a witch. One of the tests included having to recite a prayer perfectly. If the alleged witch failed to perfectly recite the prayer, they were proven to be a witch. Another test was that they would tie up the hands and feet of the accused and attach heavy rocks to the bottom, throwing them in a river or water. If they drowned and died, they were proven innocent. If they were able to float, then they were proven to be a witch, resulting in their execution. The majority of people that were accused and executed were women, but men were also accused. Cotton Mather who received his education at Harvard University, was a Minister in Salem and an

OUIJA BOARD ENIGMA

ardent and uncompassionate community leader that used his pulpit to persecute "alleged" witches. It may have been that Mather had seen magicians performing close-up magic and he confused simple illusions for "diabolical feats" aided by supernatural forces. He may have graduated at age 18 with a Master's Degree from Harvard University, but a piece of paper does not make you any more educated than does a rock. It is the human that makes the education and it is the sum of the experiences in education that make the person. There may have been one or two individuals that actually were involved in anything related to witchcraft in Salem. But it is wholly inconceivable to believe that witchcraft was somehow causing a threat to normal life in Salem. It is more likely than not, Mather saw the issue of witchcraft as a way to earn fame and to create followers. This, of course, would

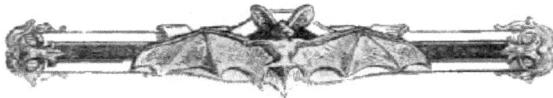

imply that he was doing it for financial gain. If he was not doing it for financial gain and the fame which brings financial gain, then why was he writing "pamphlets" denouncing witchcraft and selling them? Mather stood to gain financially for the Salem Witch Trials and it is this motive that created and drove the wholesale persecution of community members, under the guise of combating evil. The motives were purely political and economic and had nothing to do with combating spiritualism, stopping occultism, or eradicating paganism. Characteristics that could get you accused of being a witch that is working for the Devil included theft, being poor, being a woman, knowing a suspected witch, being a middle aged woman with even some type of authority, licentiousness, and many others. All of these characteristics were believed by the Puritan community of Salem as being signs that these

OUIJA BOARD ENIGMA

Cotton Mather is believed to be responsible for the
Salem Witch Trials

individuals were working with evil supernatural
forces.

OUIJA BOARD ENIGMA

MATHER

In his 1692 book titled "Memorable Providences Relating To Witchcrafts & Possessions", Cotton Mather said "In her ludicrous Fits, one while she would be for Flying; and she would be carried hither and thither, though not long from the ground, yet so long as to exceed the ordinary power of Nature in our Opinion of it: another-while she would be for Diving, and use the Actions of it towards the Floor, on which, if we had not held her, she would have thrown herself. Being at this exercise she told us, that they said, still must go down to the Bottom of our Well, for there was Plate there, and they said, they would bring her safely up again. This did she tell us, though she had never heard of any Plate there and we ourselves who had newly bought the house, hardly knew of any; but the former Owner of the House just then coming in, told

OUIJA BOARD ENIGMA

Magicians were often mistaken for sorcerers

us there had been Plate for many Years at the Bottom of the Well. She had once a great mind to have eaten a roasted Apple, but whenever she attempted to eat it, her Teeth would be set, and sometimes, if she went to take it up her Arm would be made so stiff, that she could not possibly bring her hand to her Mouth: at last she said, 'Now they say, I shall eat it, if I eat it quickly' and she nimbly eat it all up. Moreover,

OUIJA BOARD ENIGMA

there was one very singular passion that frequently attended her. An Invisible Chain would be put about her, and she, in much pain and Fear, cry out. When they began to put it on, once I did with my own hand knock it off as it began to be fastened about her. But ordinarily) When it was on, she'd be pulled out

OUIJA BOARD ENIGMA

of her seat with such violence towards the Fire, that it has been as much as one or two of us could do to keep her out. Her Eyes were not brought to be perpendicular to her feet, when she rose out of her Seat, as the Mechanism of a Human Body requires in them that rise, but she was one dragged wholly by other Hands:

OUIJA BOARD ENIGMA

and once, When I gave a stamp on the Hearth, just between her and the Fire, she screamed out, (though I think she saw me not) that I jarred the Chain, and hurt her Back."

OBSERVATIONS

1. Cotton Mather was lying. He was making up this story to get attention. Women did not fly in front of him and he said these things to get famous.

2. Cotton Mather was hallucinating from eating rotted bread. Rotting bread was a common problem in the 17th century, especially without the comforts of a refrigerator. It is logical to entertain the possibility that Mather was hallucinating about the rise of witchcraft.

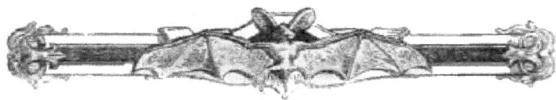

3. Cotton Mather had seen a few cases of witchcraft and had personified the issue to create a following.

4. Cotton Mather had witnessed street performers doing sleight of hand magic tricks and illusions, making him mistakenly believe that he was witnessing supernatural forces at work.

5. Mather's wholly Puritan upbringing caused him to associate witchcraft with sexuality, which might explain why the majority of the accused were women.

Any of the aforementioned observations could be the reason that Mather lead the thinking process that lead to the Salem Witch Trials. Mather had no part in the trials but his name became synonymous with the trials because his thinking mode as a community leader

OUIJA BOARD ENIGMA

influenced other influential leaders, who in turn
supported or participated in the Salem Witch

OUIJA BOARD ENIGMA

Trials. The trials are celebrated every year by tourists that flock to Salem, MA for the annual event, bringing their Ouija Boards with them to attempt to contact the spirits of the murdered. Ouija Board enthusiasts believe that the spirits of the murdered alleged "witches" are still wandering and haunting Salem. There were

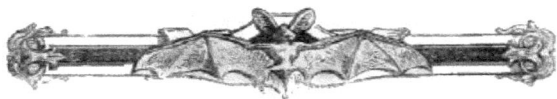

OUIJA BOARD ENIGMA

over 150 persons that were accused. Having a pet in your home was enough to get you accused of being in contract with the Devil. Some were strangled, some were hanged, some were burned at the stake, some escaped, and some confessed and in turn received pardon. May and September of 1692 were the months with the most activity. A community backlash, however quiet, did lead to the cessation of the Salem Witch Trials. One of the judges involved in the trials, even purchased land which he used to give refuge to families that had been ostracized, once the trials were over.

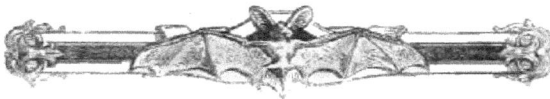

OUIJA BOARD ENIGMA

ZOZO

Zozo, also known as Pazuzu, is a unique part of the Ouija Board phenomenon. Zozo was first reported in 1816 in France, in the Dictionaire Infernal. Zozo is thought to be accompanied by the demon Mama (known in 1816 as Mimi). The many legends, urban and rural, speak about possessions which symptoms include:

    a. Headaches

    b. Nausea

    c. Abusive behavior (cursing, etc.)

    d. Hallucinations

    e. Double vision

OUIJA BOARD ENIGMA

f.   Erratic body movements

g.   Contortions of body parts

h.   Extreme anger

i.   Agitation

j.   Excessive swearing

Whether these are true or not, they have been documented in history as existing. Many legends have been documented in historical texts but this does not make them true. Like all enigmas, the Ouija Board Enigma is nearly unsolvable.

WHY IT'S UNSOLVEABLE

Science has argued that it is your ideomotor actions that are controlling the planchette on the Ouija Board, causing it to spell letters. This is a valid theory and one that is based on scientific research. The spiritualists argue that it is a spirit that you are contacting who is controlling the planchette and spelling the

OUIJA BOARD ENIGMA

OUIJA BOARD ENIGMA

letters. I tend to agree with the scientific camp more than I would with the spiritualists, but there are certain questions based on my observations that are not able to be answered by scientists. Most of the spiritualist activity up until now has copied the techniques of magicians and illusionists in order to re-create so-called supernatural effects. If there has

OUIJA BOARD ENIGMA

been spirits haunting so many different places,
where is there no footage of them in either film
or picture form? I do not doubt the existence of
spirits. But I am questioning why 7 billion
people have as of now failed to capture
substantial evidence that could prove beyond a
shadow of a doubt that spirits are causing

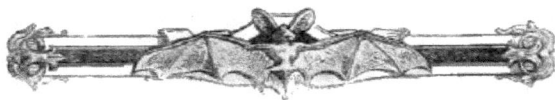

OUIJA BOARD ENIGMA

trouble. Because no concrete evidence has yet
been submitted to the public that could prove
that demon possessions take place because of
playing with a Ouija Board, the Ouija Board
has to be viewed as a toy. Owning such a thing
300 years ago could have gotten you burned at

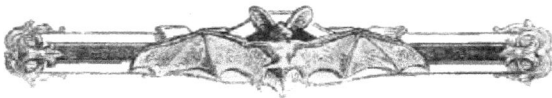

OUIJA BOARD ENIGMA

the stake or tortured or imprisoned. A United States judge in the early 1900's ruled that the Ouija Board is a sporting good and should be sold as such. Practically every toy store you enter sells a Ouija Board or a spirit board aka talking board. It is one of the bestselling board

games of all time and it is wildly popular with

OUIJA BOARD ENIGMA

people under the age of 25. Most of the people that played with the Ouija Board for the first time, did so in their youth. There are some questions that have to be answered and I have made my observations regarding use of the Ouija Board.

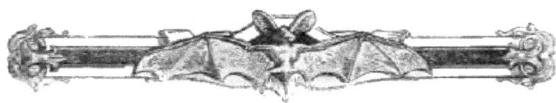

OUIJA BOARD ENIGMA

OBSERVATIONS

a. Why does the planchette move in a infinity type shape on the board? If my muscular movements are controlling it, would not my ideomotor activity cause the planchette to move directly to an

OUIJA BOARD ENIGMA

answer instead of making 3 or 4 swirls in an infinity shape before moving to the answer? Is my own ideomotor system that un-calibrated that it is not able to direct the planchette directly to the answer "Yes"?

b. The planchette speeds up and slows down. Why does the planchette speed up or slow down? Is my ideomotor activity (automatic muscular movements) increasing and decreasing?

c. Why does the Electromagnetic Frequency Meter (EMF) make noise when the planchette gets closer to it and cease making noise when the planchette gets farther from it? Why does the EMF meter raise in intensity

when my voice gets louder? The EMF meter should not get louder if there is no kinetic energy present.

d. If what the scientists claim about ideomotor activity is true and it is your mind controlling your planchette, why is it that when you ask questions about the future you receive precise answers? Does your mind control the answers to the future?

The aforementioned questions should be attempted to be explained by scientists, philosophers, and thinkers, as well as users of the Ouija Board. I tend to lean more towards a scientific explanation as to the movement of the planchette and that is ideomotor activity or automatic muscular movements. Nearly 150 years of research backs up this conclusion and

OUIJA BOARD ENIGMA

this conclusion is by far the most logical one. The Ouija Board is an enigma, an unsolved mystery that both scientists and spiritualists have to solve. However there are still unanswered questions that leave open (even the slightest) possibility that the Ouija Board could be either.

OUIJA BOARD ENIGMA

(No Model.)

E. J. BOND.
TOY OR GAME.

No. 446,054.   Patented Feb. 10, 1891.

Fig. 1.

RULES OF THE OUIJA BOARD

According to users of spirit boards aka talking boards or the Ouija Board, there are some general rules and legends about using the board and they are:

1. Never use the board alone. Supposedly, using the board alone invites unwanted spirits and demonic possession.

2. Never leave the planchette on the Ouija Board. When you are done using the

OUIJA BOARD ENIGMA

Ouija Board, take the planchette off of the board to avoid supposedly leaving open a gateway where spirits can enter.

3. Never ask the spirit to take control of you or to take control of your body or mind.

4. Placing silver on the board will stop demonic spirits from entering.

5. Using the Ouija Board opens a gateway that allows evil spirits to enter.

6. Never use the Ouija Board in a cemetery or place that could have spirits in it.

OUIJA BOARD ENIGMA

7. A cold breeze or an area suddenly becoming cold indicates the presence of a spirit.

8. The Ouija Board could be controlled by a lying spirit rather than a friendly spirit.

9. You should not anger the spirit you are talking with or there could be physical consequences.

10. The spirit you are talking to in the Ouija Board tells you about future events in a process known as "Progressive Entrapment" in order to gain your trust.

11. Throwing away the Ouija Board will not properly get rid of the spirits that are associated with it when you used it. Some believe that in order to properly

OUIJA BOARD ENIGMA

dispose of the Ouija Board, you have to break in to several pieces, sprinkle Holy Water over it, and bury it. Others believe burning it will achieve the same task.

12. Put the Ouija Board away when you are not using and make sure that the planchette and board are separated from each other.

OUIJA BOARD ENIGMA

13. Never take substances (don't do drugs, don't drink alcohol) when using the Ouija Board.

14. Burning sage clears negative energies from room. Sage was used by the Native Americans for clearing negative or evil energies.

OUIJA BOARD ENIGMA

15. Have a sound recording device to record your sessions and keep a notepad with you so that you could write down important information. This will serve as a reference to you and it is easier than attempting to remember minute details.

OUIJA BOARD ENIGMA

OUIJA BOARD GLOSSARY

Astral Projection – An experience that involves your spirit leaving your body and travelling to an astral plane.

Astrology – Fortune-telling method that uses the stars to predict the future.

Automatic Writing – Method used by spiritualists to communicate with the dead. Involves the use of a planchette with a pencil inserted in it to allow for the writing of messages by spirits. Believed by scientists to use the same ideomotor principle as the Ouija Board.

Candle – Paraffin object that emits light from a wick powered flame. Used by witches to amplify or increase the power of their spells.

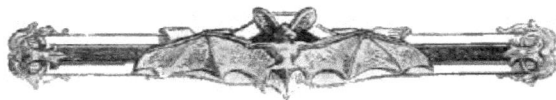

OUIJA BOARD ENIGMA

Conjuring – Art of making items appear out of thin air. Used by illusionists and magicians. Commonly mistaken for supernatural abilities.

Coven – Group of witches or association of witches.

Curran – Pearl Curran was a woman that claimed to have authored a novel based on her experiences with a spirit.

Demon – An evil or Satanic spirit.

Demonologist – Individual that specializes in the study of demons.

Dream Walking – Supposed skill by witches that allows them to enter the dreams of anyone at will.

OUIJA BOARD ENIGMA

Doyle – Sir Arthur Conan Doyle was an avid spiritualist and author of Sherlock Holmes novels.

Ectoplasm – Liquid ejected from mediums during séance.

EMF – Electromagnetic Frequency meter used to measure kinetic energy.

EVP – Electronic Voice Phenomenon. Using electronic devices to communicate with spirits.

Familiars – Pets, usually cats, under the control of witches.

Ghost – Spirit or apparition.

Ghost Hunting – Finding spirits using audio and visual recording equipment.

OUIJA BOARD ENIGMA

Grimoire – Book of spells.

Hasbro – Toy company that owns the Ouija patent and trademark.

Haunted House – A residence that is rumored to have spirits in it.

Houdini – Eric Weiss aka Harry Houdini was a famous escapologist and magician that exposed spiritualists and mediums.

Ideomotor – Automatic muscular movement caused by nonconscious mental activity.

Kennard – Charles Kennard is believed to be the creator of the modern talking board known as the Ouija Board.

OUIJA BOARD ENIGMA

Kinetic Energy – Moving energy. Also known as poltergeist in the German language.

Magicians – Illusionists that were commonly mistaken for having supernatural powers, because of their sleight of hand abilities.

Margery – Famous early 20th century medium that was exposed as a charlatan by Harry Houdini.

Mather – Cotton Mather was a Harvard trained pamphleteer that claimed to have seen witches. Mather is believed to be indirectly responsible for the creation of the Salem Witch Trials.

Mama – Demon that accompanies Zozo. Mama is also known as Mimi.

OUIJA BOARD ENIGMA

Medium – Individual that invites a spirit to control them in order to speak through them.

Occam's Razor – The simplest explanation is the most correct one.

OUIJA BOARD ENIGMA

Occult – Secret or hidden knowledge.

Oracle – A device for forecasting the future.

Ouija – Combination of the French "Oui" and German "Ja" words meaning "yes".

Paranormal – Phenomena that cannot be explained by modern science.

Parker Brothers – Toy company that purchased rights to the Ouija Board in 1966.

Planchette – Small triangular shaped wooden device used as a pointer on the Ouija Board.

Possession – Demonic control of a human by an evil spirit.

OUIJA BOARD ENIGMA

Progressive Entrapment – Deceptive process used by a spirit to establish trust with Ouija Board user.

Pseudoscience – Beliefs or claims not rooted in science.

OUIJA BOARD ENIGMA

Pythagoras – Inventor of the talking board in 540 B.C.

Sage – Native American plant used to ward off evil spirits or negative energy.

Salem Witch Trials – Trials that took place on 1692 in Salem, MA that lead to the persecution and execution of over 150 individuals, mostly female.

Samhain – Irish festival held on October 31st that marks the beginning of Winter.

Séance – Ritual used to contact a spirit of the dead.

Soothsayer – Ancient fortune-teller.

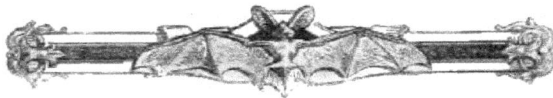

OUIJA BOARD ENIGMA

Spell – Incantation written or spoken in order to effect, change, or control a physical object (animate or inanimate).

Spiritualist – A person that uses methods such as Automatic Writing, the Ouija Board,

OUIJA BOARD ENIGMA

Séances, etc. to communicate with the dead or supernatural forces.

Talisman – Object embedded with a spell or spells giving it supernatural power.

Talking Board – Spirit Board also known as Ouija Board.

Tilly – Young girl that claimed to have been possessed by Zozo in 1816 in France.

Tituba – First Native American woman accused of witchcraft.

Voodoo – Tribal magic of African origin practiced by slaves in North America.

Witch – A pagan that uses spells and conjuring to affect their environment.

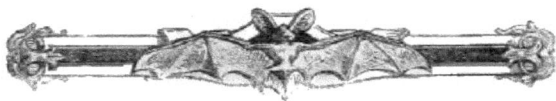

OUIJA BOARD ENIGMA

Witchboard – Popular 1980's movie based around the Ouija Board and demonic possession.

Zozo – Ancient Babylonian demon. Also known as Pazuzu.

OUIJA BOARD ENIGMA

OUIJA BOARD ENIGMA

ACKNOWLEDGMENTS

California State University Dominguez Hills

Shervin Khoramianpour

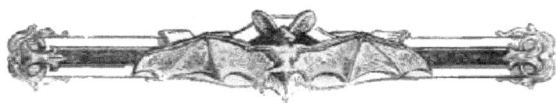

OUIJA BOARD ENIGMA

KAMBIZ MOSTOFIZADEH TITLES

Facebook.com/KambizMostofizadeh
Instagram.com/KambizMostofizadeh

OUIJA BOARD ENIGMA

NOTES

OUIJA BOARD ENIGMA

NOTES

OUIJA BOARD ENIGMA

NOTES

OUIJA BOARD ENIGMA

NOTES

OUIJA BOARD ENIGMA

NOTES

OUIJA BOARD ENIGMA

NOTES

OUIJA BOARD ENIGMA

NOTES

OUIJA BOARD ENIGMA

NOTES

OUIJA BOARD ENIGMA

NOTES

OUIJA BOARD ENIGMA

NOTES

OUIJA BOARD ENIGMA

NOTES

OUIJA BOARD ENIGMA

NOTES

OUIJA BOARD ENIGMA

NOTES

OUIJA BOARD ENIGMA

NOTES

OUIJA BOARD ENIGMA

NOTES

OUIJA BOARD ENIGMA

NOTES

OUIJA BOARD ENIGMA

NOTES

OUIJA BOARD ENIGMA

NOTES

OUIJA BOARD ENIGMA

NOTES

OUIJA BOARD ENIGMA

NOTES

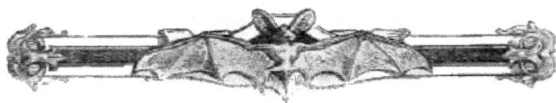